BREAKING SILENCE

Jacob Sam-La Rose was born in London in 1976. He was managing director of a web development studio before becoming a freelance writer and editor. He served as Artistic Director of the London Teenage Poetry SLAM from 2003 to 2009, and is an editor for flipped eye press. He also facilitates a range of literature-in-education, creative writing and spoken word programmes through schools, arts centres and other institutions.

His work has appeared in many anthologies and journals, including *Identity Parade: New British & Irish Poets* (Bloodaxe Books), *Poems For Love* (Penguin), *I Have Found a Song* (Enitharmon Press), *Red* (Peepal Tree), *Learn Then Burn: The Ultimate Poetry Guide for the High School or College Classroom* (Write Bloody) and Michael Rosen's *A-Z: The Best Children's Poetry from Agard to Zephaniah* (Puffin). His pamphlet *Communion* (flipped eye) was a Poetry Book Society Pamphlet Choice in 2006. *Breaking Silence* (Bloodaxe Books, 2011) is his first book-length collection.

JACOB SAM-LA ROSE

BREAKING
SILENCE

BLOODAXE BOOKS

Copyright © Jacob Sam-La Rose 2011

ISBN: 978 1 85224 915 1

First published 2011 by
Bloodaxe Books Ltd,
Highgreen,
Tarset,
Northumberland NE48 1RP.

www.bloodaxebooks.com
For further information about Bloodaxe titles
please visit our website or write to
the above address for a catalogue.

Supported by
**ARTS COUNCIL
ENGLAND**

Cover design: Neil Astley & Pamela Robertson-Pearce.

Printed in Great Britain by
Bell & Bain Limited, Glasgow, Scotland.

For Pops

ACKNOWLEDGEMENTS

Thanks are due to the editors of the following publications in which some of these poems have appeared, sometimes in different versions: *Identity Parade: New Poets from Britain and Ireland* ('The Beautiful', 'Plummeting'), *City State: New London Poetry* ('Spilling Out', 'How To Be Black', 'The Difficulty and the Beauty'), *The Barbershop Chronicles* ('Alpha'), *A Storm Between Fingers* ('Ymir'), *I Have Found a Song* ('Magnitude'), *Automatic Lighthouse* ('Never'), and *Trespass* ('Song for a Spent 100w Bulb'). Some of the poems have also been recorded by the Poetry Archive.

I would like to thank Danielle Shaw, Nii Ayikwei Parkes, Roger Robinson, Malika Booker, Peter Kahn, Suzanne Alleyne, Nathalie Teitler and Tara Betts for their support, advice and feedback. Many thanks also to the Vineyard community of poets, Dorothy Fryd, Miriam Nash and the Barbican Young Poets for continuing to keep me on my toes.

CONTENTS

IV

Song for a Spent 100w Bulb

Too bright to live long,
   too costly, my mother feared
your appetite, guzzling the mains,
   hung from the ceiling, little sun
I rhymed into, close as I could stand,
   imagining the bulbed head of a mic,
searing fistful of feverish light
   against my face – suddenly emptied,
plinked out, no longer able to beat back
   the dark, capable only of cooling
after-image, of dying
   memory, milky glass shell
and filament jangle, capable
   of being held, of being rolled
in a boy's hot palm, singing
   one soft, blind note.

I

In the darkness it's hard to tell who is listening and who is speaking.
PHILIP LEVINE, 'In the Dark'

Rapture

From the headlines of *The New York Times*
front page, James Barron reports it's judgement day
tomorrow. I'm jogging, headphones in my ears,
Friday morning in the local park and I don't feel

prepared. There's sunlight in the spaces between
the leaves, and all the other things I haven't seen
or done, but of course, none of that matters
now. I've lost track of the judgement days

incoming. My money was on 2012, the ancient
Mayan calendar. The ice shelves are falling,
our mobile phones confuse the bees,
and the mushroom clouds that overshadowed

my youth still wait offstage to do their dirty work.
Who was it that said that everyone's an atheist
until the plane goes down? Last night, a woman crossed
my path at the top of a flight of stairs and asked

if I was superstitious. I never knew that was bad luck,
but even the things you don't believe in can get you
at the end. There's the man who built a clock
in a desert, underground, designed to keep perfect time

for 10,000 years, and there's a mountain stuffed with
nuclear waste that requires a warning sign with an expiration
date pitched far beyond any languages we currently know.
And rapture, which I always believed was the sound you made

with someone's tongue at work against a private stretch
of skin, the way some part of you is carried away.
I don't know if I've done enough to make the rollcall
of the celestial spaceship some would say is coming

for them. I'd like to believe the park I'm jogging round
will still be here tomorrow, the dogs still nosing
at each other's flanks, oblivious. Jogging, which is itself
a form of prayer for an unknown future, all that moving

forward step by step. Tonight, says the man who built
the clock, the hour and minute hand will pass
the midnight mark and no one knows
how many times they've done that before.

The next song in my ears carries the line
come get me, 'cause we don't have much time left.
Perhaps our truer days of rapture or judgement
are less grand, or much more local, while

elsewhere, the world still turns.

Pendulum

The girl in reception will probably keep the baby.
The boy in the next office doesn't know what to do.
One night, after hours, you sit on a cold brick wall,
your arm around her shoulders, holding her together
as the tears come too suddenly for her to speak
and she cries into her palms, too weak to stand.
You want to help. He's not there. She calls it *love*.

It's beginning to rain as it often does in movies
at moments like this, and you don't know it yet,
but there will be phone calls. She will drag you
out of sleep, voice blurred with questions.
Hours will pass. Some nights the way she describes him
will chime with the shadows chased across your wall
by passing headlights. Days from now, she will show you
his picture in her wallet, back behind the plastic
with other important things, smiling
as if he never left. It will dizzy you.

You will learn to guarantee that nothing stays
the same, that everything moves. You will remember
a physics lesson, a teacher who spoke of constant flux,
a pendulum's swinging weight. But you won't be able
to find any way to stop that pendulum's back and forth,
any more than you can stop one minute bleeding
into the next. The best you can do now is hold her close
and strain to hear, somewhere deep inside her,
a different clock beginning to mark its own time.

The Manager's Wife

I remember how thin she was,
but I don't remember her name.
Pale, with sparse, cropped blonde hair.
Nothing like the glossy women
spread across the pages of the men's
magazines we flipped through
when shirts had been refolded
and hangers spaced evenly on rails.
On quiet days, we'd flock around the cash desk,
trying to make sense of the match.
The shop floor agreed. Something didn't add up.
Someone had made a mistake.
As managers went, ours was a nice guy.
Said nothing if you were a few minutes late
as long as you made up the time.
The wife drifted by every once in a while,
flashing a brittle smile before lunch dates
with visiting friends. There were rumours
of how much the wedding cost.
Laughing, she'd raise a hand to her mouth,
wrist angled to flaunt a stiletto-thin finger
weighted with a nugget of cool rock.
It didn't take much to see how it stretched him.
I wondered what kept him there,
alone some nights among the empty jackets
and jeans, trying to make the day's figures fit.

Conversations with Adamh

    He says
they separated when
she took to burning underwear.
She reminded him too much
of his first wife – that wildness
in her, too, the way she wouldn't
take anything lying down.

    Here, his tongue
flags. I have trouble with some
of the words. I think he says
that, of everything, the silence
worries him most; the omnipresent
silence. How, of the good old days
she was the only thing left.

    Here, my notes
are unclear – does he wish
they were together? Would he eat
everything she'd put on the table
even if he couldn't stomach the taste?
That missing rib still itches.
The pain – a welcome ache.

Never

He never taught me how to hold
a pair of clippers. I never saw him
dab cologne on his cheeks. I don't know
the smell of his sweat, or if our fingers
look alike. I didn't learn to drink
by draining whatever wine he might have left
or sharing an ice cold can. He never
wrestled me down, so I never grew up
to return the favour. I didn't learn to love
music thumbing through his vinyl LPs.
I never woke him. He never once raised
his voice at me. I never heard him laugh
and although I remember him at the end
of a long distance call, once,
I don't remember his voice
or what it might have sounded like
saying my name.

Drummer

My stepfather gave me a beating
the day I stuck my fingers in my ears
while he was talking. I didn't mean
to do it. It was an accident – first one

and then the other. My father
was a drummer. Banged out
a singular rhythm on the breakfast table
or kitchen wall (so I've been told)

to silence anything he didn't want to hear.
The blunt percussion of a weathered
palm. You had to listen. There was
a language there, between each beat.

When we finally met, he never met
my eyes. All I could do
was listen – in the moment,
that was my occupation. I grew to love

rhythm – hard pattern, how
a drum-line spoke to the soul.
The last time my mother beat me
I refused to cry. I imagined the tears

as rain on a closed window.
Plaintive rhythm, I learned
to turn it down.

Seconds

Late night, flicking through stations on the car stereo
you tune in on a rasping voice, hoisted
over lilting acoustic chords; a song
you've never heard before. The road opens up

in front of you, and there's nothing about this song
you don't already know, even down to the rasp,
the way the voice is honeyed with heartache,
the rough edge calculated to sound raw

and real. Every note is second hand.
And maybe there's some other place you need to be.
Somewhere else, where something is happening
without you, now, something so vital

that it calls out from wherever it is
and you don't know how to get there.
Maybe you're not driving. Maybe you're trying
to put words down on a blindingly blank page.

Maybe you're trying to get dressed.
Or maybe your hands are resting lightly
on the back of the neck of the person
you're supposed to love now

and maybe, for a moment,
you can't tell the difference
between that neck
and any other neck you've known.

Talk This Way

Dear boys on road,
                    dear girls on bus
top decks, dear hip-hop, dear love letters
pressed deep into vinyl platters, dear Americas,
Jamaica and East End –
                    dear Queen's best
cool and clipped as seams pressed sharp
in spite of noon day sun high in a Guyanese sky,
dear received pronunciation, dear raw, unfettered
music of my motherland once removed, dear music
smuggled in the old-fashioned way, beneath the folds
of skirts and blouses in a hard leather suitcase,
in the bones of flying fish and guava cheese,
cassava bread, in the notes of spilt casrip
loosed from broken bottles –
                    dear music
melting in the cauldron and pit, dear molten
brogue we birthed and spanked to wailing heights,
dear empty spaces, dear silence –

thank you for your many tongues.
Now, to find my own.

Make Some Noise

I said 'well daddy don't you know that things go in cycles?'
Q-TIP, 'Excursions'

Our mothers said that hip-hop wasn't music,
    that all those rappers did was talk.
Mine questioned what I heard in the hard noise
I listened to. For her, it wasn't music
    if it couldn't hold a waltz, tango or samba.
Music was something you could hold in hand,
the way a beaten steel pan begat
    a movement in the hips one night in 1953
at Tipperary Hall, east coast, and never ended.
It was Kitchener and Sparrow, Ella,
    Harry Belafonte, Bassey, Syncopators,
Washboards, Nat King Cole –
they try to tell us we're too young.
    It was the honesty of sculpted wood and steel
or nylon strung to spirituals and hymns.
It was lyric, hot and sly, and working up
    through simple instruments, piano, bass,
guitar and drum, and grew to something large
and grand, a synonym for mass.

Currency

My grandfather worked the land
     with his hands. The first job I was paid for
was Littlewoods Café. I fed a dishwasher
     cartloads of emptied plates, cups and cutlery.

I don't remember what it was worth –
     how many CDs, pairs of over-baggy Bleu Bolt jeans
or Saturday nights in clubs off Oxford Street
     those plates and hours bought me.

At 16 it was my mother who bought my ticket back
     to Guyana. The summer I'd planned with the guys
and the open purse of an empty house
     and equally empty days gave way

to a stifling heat, insects large enough
     to challenge the hand I'd threaten them with.
I spent the first seven days cursing
     the rate of exchange, the tiny melody

of mosquito wings, whatever it is
     that makes foreign blood sweet,
and I was foreign even before I opened
     my mouth. Off the ferry in Philippi,

across the Berbice river, someone pointed
     out toward an unfamiliar horizon,
finger following a line of telegraph poles
     to a vanishing point.

All of this is yours, they said, all the way
     down to the sea, which wasn't close enough
to be smelt or heard. *Your family's land.*
     Everything I could see was green –

nothing I could recognise, and things
     I didn't know how to name.

Magnitude

when I say 'night',
it is your name I am calling,
when I say 'field',
your thousand, thousand names,
your million names.

ARACELIS GIRMAY, 'Arroz Poetica'

I

There are a million grains in a 20 kilogram sack of rice.
Give or take. It's a hard enough number to imagine,

the kind that slips through the fingers, like digging
your hands in that same sack, trying to feel

for individuals; a number that surpasses
counting, bigger than the mind's computational eye

like the full, unending girth of sky, like death,
the kind of threshold you give up on

and take for granted. Imagine the sum
in eleven of those sacks and I'm trying to find a way

to make that number real, like how many pots and how long
it might take to cook that much rice and still retain the detail

of each swollen grain; a real, fleshy equation that might capture
the percentage of wastage, the amount that would fall

and be forgotten even while trying to keep count,
the appetite that might be necessary to take it all in.

II

In a lesson on trying to make the abstract more concrete,
one of my students, a Guyanese boy, late teens,

shares a draft in which he's counting
the breaths of a sleeping girlfriend.

He's met her father, shook his hand.
Weeks later, the girl explains

that her Akan blood arrows back up to royalty,
that the boy is the son of a slave,

that there is no future for them, only a past.
I understand that the counting makes it easier,

lends a sense of a narrative, a march into the future
of something as simple as breath, but it's not working.

As much as I try, I can't suggest anything
to make the poem any easier, until he offers his own

resolution: a memory of sitting on the seawall in Georgetown,
facing the Atlantic, following darts of sunlight riding

the backs of waves, wondering where each began,
how each follows the heels of another as they furl

towards wall or shore, how he can only understand
as much of it as his eye can drink in,

how the rest, for him, is a mystery.

Ymir

Imagine you are him. His arms and breath are yours
    and one long night, while sleeping, you are
pulled apart, torn into pieces like confetti

    thrown to the wind. You become a world.
One eye always shining while the other sleeps.
    Your skull is full of air, your flesh becomes

the ground that others walk upon, your bones
    are broken and remade as mountains,
teeth dug out for rocks, and for a while you think

    you might wake up and pull yourself together,
rise and walk away, but you no longer own your feet
    and toes. You learn to speak without a tongue.

When you sigh, your breath makes leaves and branches sing,
    but no one listens to your voice.
Tell me, how do you feel? Imagine you are him.

    Your heart still beats but it's called something else now.
You dream in colours, black and sky blue.
    In time you'll forget your own name.

How To Be Black

There's a little of you in everything,
and always someone trying to muscle in
on the act, trying to be the new you.

Mostly, you're cool about it, but
all the attention gets tired real quick –
eyes peering in, eager to strip you back,
layer by layer, until there's nothing left.

Deep down, people fear
there's more of you around than they
can swallow, but by the same token

there's always someone trying to ape you
like a bootlegged Gucci. *Go 'head*, you say,
*shine as hard as you like. See if I don't
ball my cheeks 'n' blow your light bulb out.*

That shadow gig's just a day job.
Mostly, you work nights.

A Song for Kung-Fu

Who didn't dream of fluency
    of muscle and bone, that jazzy language
of chops and blocks, to be the scholar
    of punch and joint lock, genius
of back flip and take down, to know how
    to move, how to stand, solo, against an army
of hands and feet intent on ending you;
    to take a beating and be redeemed,
to slough off your softer flesh and come back
    stronger, reborn as iron shirt, crane or tiger,
capable of solving the math of any problem
    with knuckles, palms or heels?

Keeping Up

New Cross. We found a court on a backstreet, hungry
for new ground, eager to test our game against
no one we really knew. Not that any of us

was ever that good. Under a pestle of midday sun,
one kid cut through us with a crossover fade, smooth
as any girl's pressed hair. Two steps, up and away,

kissing the ball with his fingers, feeding it through
the hoop. Few things I remember as beautiful.
We stopped, hands on hips, faces twisted

from the effort of trying to keep up, to stop him
from rising. The distance brayed. He belonged
to the air, to the idea of something we were trying to be,

brought it close enough to touch, and passed us again
and again. We praised him with a chorus of ragged breath.
Him, already pulling the ball back for the next play.

Alpha

You want to be him.
Him with the mirror-shine shoes. Him
with the jacket and smile – perfect
slabs of enamel. You want
his rugged chin. His tousled coiffure,
        not a hair out of place.
You wonder if he's ever suffered rebellious
cuticles or feet that sweat, a niggling
pain in his left knee. Him
with the lips and shark-fin jaw.
        You ache to be him, him
with the ripped deltoids and pecs,
him with the extra leg-room, him
with the watch and the bottle,
the body cut from stone.
        You'd like to zip yourself
into him, to put him on and never
take him off. To tell stories
of the sex you had last night
as him, which will be believed
        in his name. For him,
heads will turn, eyes will catch and breath
will be unlatched. He who can enter
any home unchallenged.
        He who wears everything well,
who finishes first, well-fed
and satisfying.

The Negro Entrepreneur Recounts His First Enterprise

To put it plain –
                I pimped
my 'fro. And business was good.
I had off days, of course,
but soon came back in fashion.
For a premium, I'd pose
                        for portraits,
flash my pearly whites, high beam, or screw
my brow into a threat,
a full-strength pout,
with all the
        watchu talkin' 'bout, Willis?
I could muster.

I claimed to be as alien
as you'd ever know.
        Roll up!
in my best salesman's patter,
        Come One,
        Come All!
                to touch, for fee,
black woolly curls, thick
as cotton.
I learned my trade from Venus,
Huey, Malcolm.
                If you can't beat them,
        make them pay.

After Lazerdrome, McDonalds, Peckham Rye

*What's clear, now, is / that there was music, that it's lasted, that it /
doesn't matter whether a player played it, / or whether it just played itself,
that it still is / playing, / that at least two gods exist...*

ABDULAH SIDRAN, 'A Dispute About God'

where I say goodbye to south-east London for the next 3 years
a gaggle of us   still damp   spilling in from the night before

early flock for a Sunday   six or seven A.M.   sleepless
drowning in light and all this quiet   after all that sweat
and darkness   all that flighty noise

this is the year one of the guys says music is the one thing
that won't ever let him down   that music is his religion

the year we're stopped and searched because we
fit the description   the year jungle music passes
out of fashion   stripped down

to naked beat and bass   and we club together   to dance
alone   in the dark   let the music play us   meat and bone

let music fill the empty spaces   rhythm in wads and scads
scattershot   crashing   wall to wall   to be baptised
by filtered drums   pressed snares and swollen b-lines

be baptised by city songs   urban hymns   seamless
sound   a brimming sea of sound   poured out

from towering speaker stacks   this is the year we stand
close enough   to feel the music   rise   its wing-beats
on our faces   drawing salt from our skin   released

then morning   small fries and a strawberry milkshake
counting coins for the cab back   sitting around a table

slouching in moulded seats   drowning in silence
light-headed   leavened   waiting
for the right moment to move

awake for too long   ears
still ringing   drum-drunk

eyes still adjusting to the light
a weight coming down

Communion

Make the music with your mouth, Biz!
BIZ MARKIE

Street corner spotlights, cupped hands,
spit-crossed palms: solid air pressed
through teeth and lips into high-hats,
kicks, snares and even bass; the moment
passed round like a chalice or smoke
and riding it all, always, someone
with a need to be heard.

Speechless

I

At 15, she has a voice like ripe Jamoon wine
and her name is on everyone's lips.
1950. Uruguay beats Brazil 2-1

to win the World Cup, China invades Tibet,
Truth or Consequences debuts on American
television, and her father forbids her

from playing her guitar, hoists it up
on a wall between pictures of Ella Fitzgerald,
King George and a poster proclaiming

that Britain needs you. It will hang there, souvenir
of the freedom she enjoyed since she was nine
and spent three months learning to play

My Home Is Heaven Just Waiting For Me,
three simple gospel chords, in secret,
taught by her Sunday School teacher,

before unveiling her voice one evening
in front of the family. Her father stayed silent then,
but he's Police Sergeant on the Demerara's

west bank, with a sharp, black serge uniform
and standards to match. And I'd like to know how
the cogs and wheels turn in his head,

how the decision is made, whether
he weighs her tears and pleas against
the notion that a father knows best,

that his word is law, that a proper young
Guyanese woman belongs to the home
behind curtains, not music. I'd like to know

if it's just that easy. Easy as lifting
a gramophone's needle from a groove,
closing a door, or blowing out a candle.

He forbids her from playing guitar,
forbids her from singing, orders her
to fold her voice down into a small,

pocketable silence. Hangs the guitar from a nail
on a wall like a trophy or stuffed animal,
like something he's hunted and killed.

Weeks will pass, before whatever's left inside her
rises, claws its way out – before she stands on a chair,
unhooks that guitar from its resting place, brings it down

with an overhead swing that cracks the frame,
again and again, until it's broken wood, tangled nylon,
a few snagged keys.

                    The girl will be my mother.

When she tells the story, it's just a guitar.
You don't have to make it sound so bad, she'll say –
he loved us in his own, stiff way.

II

1984. Torvill and Dean score 12 perfect 6.0s
and Olympic gold, Jesse Jackson botches

a presidential campaign, half a million people
protest the regime of Ferdinand Marcos,

astronauts make the first untethered space walk
and I attend singing lessons every Saturday morning.

I've been promised the freedoms
my mother never had, so there's

choir and tap shoes, jazz hands, pianos
and Saturdays, learning to sing.

We're taught to shape mouths to tame
voices, taught chorus and harmony,

how to turn on a smile for an audience,
each bright rictus like an artificial flower.

Sometimes a new kid bursts out into tears
and we carry on singing around him.

One afternoon, after class, on the drive
to Brixton market for Saturday shopping,

we pass a skate park. For a short moment,
I'm silent, pressed up against the car's window

watching boys on their BMX bikes, one planing
up from a dip with a wild whooping holler,

handle bars twisted and limbs at brazen
angles, front wheel spinning free,

testing gravity's leash, blazing against the sky.

IV

By the time Dante's born again
    and denounces hip-hop
        as the devil's music,

I find it hard to avoid
    his wide, open mouth
        and fierce, scattered glare,

almost ready to believe
    in anything built on a fervent desire
        for salvation.

We touch fists at a bus stop in Brockley
    and for minutes, I suffer
        his depth of conviction,

the fine layer of ash on his skin –
    The tongue also is a fire, a world
        of evil among the parts of the body.

I've known many types of silence:
    the emptiness after a 6th Form lesson
        when a teacher suggests

that the world we've grown into
    won't ever allow us to be free,
        or the phone call I get

when a girlfriend is raped,
    or the night on the walk back
        from the party in Eltham when

nigger
    is launched from a passing car window
    like a slow motion bullet.

There are words that won't fit
   into verses and rhymes,
      and I know

there are silences I'll break
   and be broken by,
      and as Dante walks on,

I offer a devotion of my own:
   Grant me a tongue
      worthy of the weight

of everything I'll come to know.
   Tell me I'll write
      and write.

V

The windows look out on open school grounds
and already, before I've begun to speak
or even know their names, they're out there

on the pitch, or up in the clouds – anywhere
but here. Their teachers have said that this
is a valuable opportunity to learn

but ask the boy face down on the desk
as if its surface is a requisite for breathing,
or the three girls squealing something

I don't understand, and the rest of them
proclaiming boredom, a preference for
the Rock Club project up the hall,

Hangman, anything other than poetry
because poetry means writing, and writing
is *long, man* – so say the ones that can be bothered

to speak. *We're the dumb kids, sir*,
says one. *Why did they give you to us?*

Before the end of this lesson, the girl that lacks
patience to raise her hand before speaking
will compare herself to a broken slot machine

in the basement of a pub, inside out
and forgotten in the widening fissure
between her parents.

The boy with a desk for a face
will write of depression in a black
and beautiful light, detailing a warm,

dark pool that whispers your name.
I'll scribe for a boy who will refuse to write,
ask questions and write his answers down:

Bangladesh, a red Honda generator,
how there's nothing like family,
nothing like home, regardless of heat

when the air-con kicks out.
I'll cherish the look on his face
when I read back his words and see

a clean, unarguable flame behind his eyes,
how he's never heard himself sound like this before
and never thought it could sound so good.

Spilling Out

What's the half-life of a bright idea?
How deep must it be buried
to prevent it radiating,

like trying to stop a bulb's
insistent light from spilling out
between the fingers or leavening
the enforced blindness
of closed eyelids?

Imagine rolling that hot bulb
on your tongue,
all it's brilliant shining.

Now, try closing your mouth.

IV

Come home.
The earth utters
  to the body, and so the body does
  – come home – at last.

DAVID BAKER, 'The Rumor'

The Buddha of Miracles

(with thanks to David Shumate)

Every miracle has its science. It takes hard thought to be
original – not just another Jesus on a breadstick or the
Virgin Mother's silhouette behind a waterfall. And never
resurrecting the dead or anything that would make a yoke
for the back. Not again. He sweats. It's hard work to put it
all together, kissing shattered limbs so they blossom once
more into function after they were told to stay put. Hail
Mary. Let the ordinary births care for themselves. There
are always bigger fish to snag, unhook and bless with new
beginnings. Because everyone deserves at least one nudge back
in the right direction. It's the science of it he dreams of –
the cogs and wheels he whispers to beneath the unforgiving
surfaces of the everyday. It never matters what's really real,
only ever what's believed.

Breath

Before his legs gave way
and he went down,
straight down, as if felled

by a hard cross to the jaw,
he called her name, his body
giving in to its own weight.

A nearby nurse said *stroke*.
That same night, stretched out
on a hotel bed, my mother kept

a vigil, hand cupped over
his nose and mouth. He slept
like death, she said.

An Undisclosed Fortune

My mother's fond of the story in which
she sucks the mucus from my tiny nostrils
so I can breathe. I tried to coax

a poem from it: pictured her, breathing
life back into me like a god. The poem failed,
but came back to me while watching *E.R.*,

a resident sprayed with a patient's
pancreatic ooze, another's fingers wrapped
around a heart to coax spent muscle into

systole, diastole. I hear the same whisper
facing myself in the mirror, channelled
through the single grey hair I know is there

but lose track of, the bruise on my hip
that came from nowhere but had me limping
for days: reminders that each day is a coin

from an undisclosed fortune, that while
I've never held my lover's heart in my hands,
never had to stem loosed and wayward blood,

or force breath back into place,
one day, it might come to this.

Whatever You Can Afford

The brochure says it'll cost a thousand pounds
to bury your father's remains. He's been burned

down to ash, now there's a price list and
something distasteful about picking his plaque

or the vase with numbers attached. The truth is
you don't have enough banked for those numbers

not to mean anything. That stone equals
a month's rent, two thirds of a new computer

to replace the one that just died, the one you use
for work, to pay the bills. Today, you didn't work.

You woke with a head full of dead-ends
and elsewhere there was industry:

the sound of machinery earning return
on investment in the garage behind the house,

a breeze muscling through nearby trees,
the drunks communing on the corner.

It's one of those days when you want to give in,
or give up, however it's said. You'd like to believe

you could trade in whatever you have: electricity on tap,
a small army of screens to wash your face with light

and all the other modern conveniences, a roof
over your head, four walls to be hemmed in by;

you'd like to believe you could give it all up
for an honest patch of dirt, things that cost no more

than you can pay for with bare hands,
a clear patch of sky you can borrow from God

and call your own for as long as you wish.

How To Be Gravity

Be a mammy.

Fleshy arms unwilling to let anything go
and always someone fighting your grip,
trying
      to muster enough speed to escape you.

Enforce the rules with the palm of your hand.
Moonlight as death
                 or a jealous god.

Put heaven and hell in their place.

Know that there are more intimate places
to hook your anchors
than flesh or bone.

There's a part of everyone
that will always escape you
                 at the end.

Until then, pull everything
          down,
      down,
down.

Plummeting

He works it, ear accustomed to the tune
of hard play: left, right, launch-step, discipline like a lump

of lead in his pocket he can melt
into gold. Keeps on until the sky turns plum,

sporting a corona of sweat like a plume
of peacock's feathers, stoking the fire in each lung

as proof against the failing light and time
passing; left, right, launch-step, pelting

ball at hoop, deep bone-ache for the sweet line
from hand to flawless, unimpeachable plunge.

The rim's wide mouth, mute.

The Other End of the Line

After he passed, my mother spoke about him
as if he were still there. She complained
if he didn't come to her in dreams.
You haven't gone to see him yet, she said,
meaning it had been some time since
I'd stood over his grave. For me, there was more
silence. The telephone receiver off the hook,
no one there at the other end of the line.
The person you are trying to reach
is currently unavailable, said the automated
voice. And there was so much left to say.

A Spell for Forgetting a Father

He was whole years, Son
& even at this moment,
he walks through your face

TERRANCE HAYES
'Mother to Son' (*Hip Logic*)

For this spell you will need candles, feathers
and your own strong head for heights.

Find a place in full view of the sun. Before dawn,
inscribe your father's name on each candle. Light them

while repeating your own name under your breath.
Wax each feather's nib; lay them on the ground

to form a pair of wings. Your wings can be as ornate
or as simple as you wish. Keep the largest feather in hand.

As the sun's light strengthens, lie back so the wings
meet your shoulders. Imagine them powerful, beating

against air, lifting your full weight. Hold the largest feather
above you so its shadow falls on your face; say

as I release you
so you release me.

Let the feather fall. When you are finished
leave that feather on the ground. Bury the rest.

Here, Spirits

When a jot of noodle meets the table,
    escapee from the chopsticks raised
to your mouth, I say the spirits are hungry:

what my aunt would say
    whenever food was dropped.
You're feeding spirits, boy,

for the plate of rice
    that hit the kitchen floor –
some solid form of libations, offerings.

Hard to shift the image of phantom mouths
    wreathed round the ankles, each deft nudge
to divert loaded forks or spoons.

It's years since I heard the story
    of the uncle who woke my mother up
to turn the television on,

switch channel to a title bout
    though he'd passed three days before.
What the spirits want, they know to take or ask for.

You challenge my first thought with more, a pea
    for a prayer of security,
a tear of chicken for provision,

a fleck of carrot for nothing.
    And the noodle?
A prayer for you.

The Difficulty and the Beauty

Who speaks of victory? To endure is everything.
RAINER MARIA RILKE

Sometimes, it's like fishing, perched
on the bank of a body of water
that ripples out to an indifferent horizon.

There's a part of you casting a line
that disappears beneath the water's surly face,
and waiting. Always the business

of waiting – no guaranteed reward beyond
the hook in your gut that pulls you back
to this same place, time and again;

whatever whispers in your ear to cast out
longer, deeper still, in spite of all the junk
that you return: the Coke cans, boots and small fries

blindly snagged and hauled into unforgiving light.
There are days when you wonder
what this so-called work is worth,

this clean-handed trawling of depths,
this wealth of time spent, marked
by the furl and slap of each collapsing wave

like the turning of the next, blank page.
Sometimes, it's an empty bucket,
or the simple currency of a sunset, brazen

as the sugars in autumn leaves. Sometimes
it's the distant light of stars and peopled windows
that your eyes expand to hold. And sometimes

it's the next real tug on the line,
the day's catch reeling in.

An Ordinary Prayer

I sometimes imagine that, one day,
we'll meet. Maybe in a café for lunch.
You'll be someone I never expected:

a 12 year old boy crowned with the nimbus
of an imperfect afro, perhaps a single mother
with serene eyes and too many mouths to feed,

a waiter on break, or a curt businesswoman
in heels and trouser suit, married to the job.

Sitting there, clear view on an open street,
an early evening, the window beginning to fill,
I'll remember all the other times I've wished

that you were there. Times I've asked you
to forgive the regular lapses, grey days and slumps.
Times I've asked you to protect me from myself,

from the occasional pain in my chest,
the strands of blood in the toothpaste and spit,

and all the dark futures ripening beneath my skin.
The times I've asked you to protect me from
falls, my shortening breath, the weight of all the days

strung behind me like cans streaming behind
a wedding car. Times I've asked you to protect me
from numbers, to sweet-talk probability, plug

your finger in the eager barrel of a loaded gun
on my behalf, catch the hammer before it strikes.

Facing me, you'll sip from a cup, lay it down,
and all at once I'll take in the darkening
corners of the room, the map of stains

on the table's surface, that the seat I'm in
was warm when I sat down. I've imagined
the moment ending in many different ways,

but mostly, when I look up,
you're gone.

NOTES

James Byrd Jnr (31)
James Byrd Jnr was an African-American murdered on 7th June 1998 in Texas. Three men dragged Byrd behind a pick-up truck for three miles before dumping his torso in front of an African-American cemetery. The following morning, Byrd's limbs were found scattered across a seldom-used road. The police found 75 places that were littered with Byrd's remains. Byrd's lynching-by-dragging gave impetus to passage of a Texas hate crimes law.

Ymir (32)
In Norse mythology, Ymir was the first frost giant, killed by the three sons of Borr, his own descendants. Odin, Vili and Vée used parts of Ymir's lifeless body to create the universe.

Speechless, IV (50)
Lines 14-15 are drawn from the Bible, James 3:6.

Plummeting (63)
The poem follows a form put forward by Terrance Hayes in his collection *Hip Logic*, which proposed poems of 11 lines, the word at the end of each line drawn from letters contained within the title. Those ending words should be of no less that four letters.